Born in Liverpool in 1945, Vincent Nichols studied for the priesthood in Rome. He was ordained in 1969 for the Archdiocese of Liverpool and then served parishes in Wigan and Toxteth. In 1992, he became an auxiliary bishop to Westminster and then Archbishop of Birmingham in 2000. In 2009, he was installed as the eleventh Archbishop of Westminster and welcomed Pope Benedict during the papal visit to the UK in 2010. On 22 February 2014, he was created Cardinal by Pope Francis.

In addition to being patron of a number of Catholic charities, including the Passage and the Cardinal Hume Centre, Cardinal Nichols is the first Chancellor of St Mary's University, Twickenham. Recently, he launched the Santa Marta Group to combat human trafficking and opened Bakhita House in London, a refuge for survivors of this appalling crime.

Cardinal Nichols is acknowledged as a strong campaigner for the vulnerable in society and a leading advocate for interfaith cooperation and integration. He is also a keen, lifelong fan of Liverpool Football Club.

THE GLORY OF THE CROSS

A journey through
Holy Week and Easter

Cardinal Vincent Nichols

First published in Great Britain in 2019

Society for Promoting Christian Knowledge
36 Causton Street
London SW1P 4ST
www.spck.org.uk

British Library Cataloguing-in-Publication Data
A catalogue record for this book is available from the British Library

ISBN 978–0–281–08197–4
eBook ISBN 978–0–281–08198–1

1 3 5 7 9 10 8 6 4 2

Typeset by Manila Typesetting Company
Printed in Great Britain by Jellyfish Print Solutions

eBook by Manila Typesetting Company

Produced on paper from sustainable forests

Contents

Contents

Part 4
LIFE FROM THE TOMB (EASTER SUNDAY)

Introduction

In this book I invite you to join me on a pilgrimage, as together we accompany the Lord on his journey through suffering, death and resurrection.

As we walk together on this pilgrimage, there is an image I would like you to keep in mind. It is a vivid image, and it comes to us from the story of the Exodus: the journey of the ancient Israelites from their slavery in Egypt to the freedom of the promised land. It is a journey that represents our pilgrimage through life.

The image I have in mind comes from the Old Testament Book of Numbers, which tells us how the Israelites complained to Moses in the wilderness because they could find no water.

> Then Moses and Aaron gathered the assembly together before the rock, and he said to them, 'Hear now, you rebels: shall we bring water for you out of this rock?' And Moses lifted up his hand and struck the rock with his staff twice, and water came out abundantly, and the congregation drank, and their livestock.
>
> (Numbers 20.10–11)

This life-giving water came from the rock face as a gift of God, a gift that not only saved the people and their cattle from the thirst that tormented them, but also gave them hope and promise for the rest of their journey.

In our lives, we too come up against many rock faces. But we shall see how the promise of Jesus, through the action of the Holy Spirit, can break open each solid rock that we face so that it becomes a spring of living water. This is the Easter mystery, the story of our salvation, which we enter, celebrate, enact and receive again each year in Holy Week.

Part 1

WATER FROM THE ROCK
(PALM SUNDAY)

1

Jesus enters the city

When [Jesus] drew near to Bethphage and Bethany, at the mount that is called Olivet, he sent two of the disciples, saying, 'Go into the village in front of you, where on entering you will find a colt tied, on which no one has ever yet sat. Untie it and bring it here. If anyone asks you, "Why are you untying it?" you shall say this: "The Lord has need of it."' So those who were sent went away and found it just as he had told them. And as they were untying the colt, its owners said to them, 'Why are you untying the colt?' And they said, 'The Lord has need of it.' And they brought it to Jesus, and throwing their cloaks on the colt, they set Jesus on it. And as he rode along, they spread their cloaks on the road. As he was drawing near – already on the way down the Mount of Olives – the whole multitude of his disciples began to rejoice and praise God with a loud voice for all the mighty works that they had seen, saying, 'Blessed is the King who comes in the name of the Lord! Peace in heaven and glory in the highest!'

(Luke 19.29–38)

St Luke's account of the triumphant procession of Jesus and his disciples tells us that they set off from near the Mount of Olives, along the path going down to the city. Anyone who has been to the Holy Land will know that it is a steep downward path indeed.

Jesus is entering the city. At first it seems a moment of triumph. But we know that it will soon turn into a time of opposition, of ridicule, of antagonism, of arrest, torture and death. In some ways the city is the solid rock, the obstacle that seems to stand, immobile, with its rules and its culture, directly in the path of the Lord and the proclamation of the gospel. Yet this is a rock face that Jesus has come to strike and from which he produces that stream of clear, refreshing water.

Every unyielding rock face that we encounter has already been faced by our Lord. The Gospel tells us that he has faced the betrayal of Judas, one of his chosen few, and the denial of Peter, whom he appointed as their leader. This is heartbreaking, the kind of rock that can lay us low. But Jesus accepts it, for he has the power to strike that rock and bring forth from it new and living water.

Every unyielding rock face that we encounter has already been faced by our Lord

How is this done? Remember his words from the cross. There he is, at the centre of the harshest realities of life, with those who are his executioners and with those who have become rough and dangerous men, robbers and bandits. They represent the worst of our world. Yet they stand for us all. And what does Jesus say of them? 'Father, forgive them, for they know not what they do' (Luke 23.34). And then, 'Truly, I say to you, today you will be with me in Paradise' (Luke 23.43).

In those words, the staff strikes the rock. At that moment we are asked to see all that is around us through new eyes. We are invited to look again at those whom we know and whom we think of as lost, coarsened by the habits of our city and far from the touch of grace.

In our rocky world the water does not seem to flow. Yet it is there, way below that seemingly barren surface. The water of God's grace has gone underground, yet it still rises to give flower to human goodness, generosity and sacrifice in so many places.

As we attend to the Lord, we can begin to see with his eyes, judge with his insight and respond with his tenderness and love. Jesus enters our city. He comes into our secular culture. His is a transforming presence. He strikes the rock and brings forth water. With him we begin to see how the work of God goes forward, flowing in the goodness of so many, in the worthiness of their efforts for others, in their generosity and self-sacrifice for good causes, in their desire to forgive and heal so that others may live again.

The work of striking this rock and bringing forth its water is part of a costly journey, and it will bring us face to face with the hardness of our own hearts and with the ultimate, unyielding rock of death itself. But now we sense and see the victory of Christ in his entry into the city, and our calling is to sing 'Hosanna!'

Our task is to raise our voices and to rejoice in all human goodness. By our words and actions we are to proclaim that this goodness is a reason for all people to praise God in prayer.

Praise to you, O Christ. You are the king of eternal goodness and eternal glory. Praise to you, O Christ! Amen.

2

Looking up to Jesus

Now among those who went up to worship at the feast were some Greeks. So these came to Philip, who was from Bethsaida in Galilee, and asked him, 'Sir, we wish to see Jesus.' Philip went and told Andrew; Andrew and Philip went and told Jesus. And Jesus answered them, 'The hour has come for the Son of Man to be glorified. Truly, truly, I say to you, unless a grain of wheat falls into the earth and dies, it remains alone; but if it dies, it bears much fruit. Whoever loves his life loses it, and whoever hates his life in this world will keep it for eternal life. If anyone serves me, he must follow me; and where I am, there will my servant be also. If anyone serves me, the Father will honour him.

'Now is my soul troubled. And what shall I say? "Father, save me from this hour"? But for this purpose I have come to this hour. Father, glorify your name.' Then a voice came from heaven: 'I have glorified it, and I will glorify it again.' The crowd that stood

there and heard it said that it had thundered. Others
said, 'An angel has spoken to him.' Jesus answered,
'This voice has come for your sake, not mine. Now is
the judgement of this world; now will the ruler of this
world be cast out. And I, when I am lifted up from
the earth, will draw all people to myself.' He said this
to show by what kind of death he was going to die.

(John 12.20–33)

As we join the Lord in Jerusalem, we look up to him
as 'your king' who 'is coming to you; righteous and
having salvation is he' (Zechariah 9.9), and we follow
him with joy.

All through Holy Week, Jesus is held before us, lifted up for all to see. So let us keep in mind, as a refrain,
these words of our Lord: 'I, when I am lifted up from
the earth, will draw all people to myself' (John 12.32).
Jesus is lifted up before us, first on to a donkey and
then, at the end of his journey, on to a cross.

On his entry into Jerusalem, we see him heralded,
praised, welcomed and acclaimed by his disciples and
the crowd. We learn from these events about discipleship, about what it really means to be a follower of
Jesus.

The first thing we learn is that the crowds do not understand very much about Jesus or what it means to follow him. We recognize, too, how much we have to learn, to absorb each day about the true depth and implications of being a disciple.

So we take our lesson from the words of Isaiah: 'Morning by morning he awakens; he awakens my ear to hear as those who are taught' (Isaiah 50.4). This is what we are to do: to start each day by giving our full attention to the Lord, by listening deeply for his presence and his prompts for us and by offering him our first thoughts and prayers.

The second lesson we learn is how easy it is for discipleship to be put aside. Disciples, we learn, are fickle, easily distracted. They fall asleep out

Sometimes our discipleship is only skin deep

of weariness; they erupt into arguments and jealousy; Judas betrays Jesus to his face; Peter denies he has ever known him.

This is our story too. Sometimes our discipleship is only skin deep. We too get weary with the whole enterprise; we too lapse into argument about who is to do what; we too hide our faith for convenience or comfort's sake.

Yet there are pictures here of great faithfulness too: Joseph of Arimathea comes in all hesitancy and fear to claim the body of Jesus; the women return to care for his body, anointing it with oil and with their love. That is how we, too, try to be.

As we face these truths of our discipleship, we need not be afraid, either of our failures or of our Lord. As the Lord is held before us, whether on a donkey or on the cross, he is the face of the Father's mercy. Within the embrace of this mercy we can truly renew and deepen our discipleship, step by step becoming true friends of Jesus.

There is for us in the gospel a portrait of mercy which is so helpful. It is focused on Simon Peter and his conversation with Jesus. Simon is told by Jesus that he will be sifted 'like wheat' (Luke 22.31). Yes, Simon will be tested by all that is about to happen, and we know that he will deny all knowledge of Jesus.

We too let go of the Lord when tested or sorely tried by circumstances. We too let go of him and turn to other sources of hope. But here we must listen to the next words of Jesus. He says to Simon, 'I have prayed for you that your faith may not fail' (Luke 22.32).

Yes, this applies to us too. Jesus says to each one of us, especially at the moments we find most difficult, 'I have prayed for you, Vincent, Helen, Robert, Marie, Peter . . . that your faith may not fail.'

Then, Jesus says to Simon, 'And when you have turned again, strengthen your brothers' (Luke 22.32). God's mercy is given not only to forgive and comfort us, but also to set us more fully on the road of service towards one another. Here is the true purpose of the loving mercy of God.

Loving God, may we embrace your mercy, the gift of him who is lifted up before us, that we may see and follow him more closely, day by day. Amen.

3

Following Jesus

If there is any encouragement in Christ, any comfort from love, any participation in the Spirit, any affection and sympathy, complete my joy by being of the same mind, having the same love, being in full accord and of one mind. Do nothing from rivalry or conceit, but in humility count others more significant than yourselves. Let each of you look not only to his own interests, but also to the interests of others. Have this mind among yourselves, which is yours in Christ Jesus, who, though he was in the form of God, did not count equality with God a thing to be grasped, but made himself nothing, taking the form of a servant, being born in the likeness of men. And being found in human form, he humbled himself by becoming obedient to the point of death, even death on a cross. Therefore God has highly exalted him and bestowed on him the name that is above every name, so that at the name of Jesus every knee should bow, in heaven and on earth and under the earth, and every tongue confess that Jesus Christ is Lord, to the glory of God the Father.

(Philippians 2.1–11)

We began our journey through Holy Week with Jesus' entry into Jerusalem. This event took place at the Feast of the Passover, when Jerusalem and all the surrounding countryside was packed with pilgrims coming to fulfil their duties of temple worship. We remember the shout that went up: 'Blessed is he who comes in the name of the Lord' (John 12.13). The crowd saw in Jesus one chosen by God to fulfil their hopes.

Now we have truly entered Holy Week, and we can look ahead to the events of Thursday and Friday, through which the true identity of Jesus will be made clear. We will move, rather rapidly, from the joyful shouts of Palm Sunday to the reality of the passion of our Lord, to the suffering, the self-emptying, that it demanded.

St Paul tells us the story of Jesus in this way: his state was divine, he assumed the condition of a slave, even to accepting death, but God raised him high. So now we know what is to be done: all beings should bend the knee at the name of Jesus. Now we have another shout: not, 'Blessed is he who comes in the name of the Lord', but, 'Jesus Christ is Lord, to the glory of God the Father.'

This is the truth of the One whom we follow. He is not simply someone chosen by God, someone who speaks to us of God, but he is the Lord, the One in whom the Godhead fully dwells, the divine being come into our midst.

This seriously changes everything. For once, there is an action of a human person which is also, fully and unequivocally, the action of God. For once, the human and the divine have come together in a decisive moment. This means that Jesus' victory over death, accomplished only by the power of God, is ours too; Jesus' victory over the corrosion of sin, accomplished by the power of God's love, is also ours. This victory comes to us through God in Jesus because he has fully embraced our humanity and taken it into this struggle and, in the victory, brings back to us our humanity, healed and entire.

This is why we proclaim, 'At the name of Jesus, all beings should bend the knee.' Through him, we can see our way out of the darkness, and we know that, if we stay with him, we will have a new energy, a new power to carry us through.

Victory comes to us through God because he has fully embraced our humanity

Throughout the rest of our journey, we shall ponder the marvellous ways in which the human and the divine come together, uniquely, in Jesus. It is like two elements which, when combined, create great energy. Here is an astonishing synergy that breaks open the mystery of God, making clear God's closeness and God's inner life.

This moment of synergy also transforms our understanding of ourselves and makes clear the eternal destiny to which we are called. No longer are we an excitable crowd, running after the latest self-proclaimed guru, but now we are disciples of clear intent and freedom of heart, focused on the one person, Jesus, who can lift us beyond our uncertainty and welcome us into the tender mercy of God.

O Lord, may we follow you wholeheartedly, taking each step in union with you, giving you our hearts, for truly you are Lord, to the glory of God the Father. Amen.

Part 2

LIGHT FROM DARKNESS
(MAUNDY THURSDAY)

4

Jesus washes the disciples' feet

Now before the Feast of the Passover, when Jesus knew that his hour had come to depart out of this world to the Father, having loved his own who were in the world, he loved them to the end. During supper, when the devil had already put it into the heart of Judas Iscariot, Simon's son, to betray him, Jesus, knowing that the Father had given all things into his hands, and that he had come from God and was going back to God, rose from supper. He laid aside his outer garments, and taking a towel, tied it round his waist. Then he poured water into a basin and began to wash the disciples' feet and to wipe them with the towel that was wrapped round him. He came to Simon Peter, who said to him, 'Lord, do you wash my feet?' Jesus answered him, 'What I am doing you do not understand now, but afterwards you will understand.' Peter said to him, 'You shall never wash my feet.' Jesus answered him, 'If I do not wash you, you have no share with me.' Simon Peter said to him, 'Lord, not my feet only but also my hands and my head!' Jesus said to him, 'The one who has bathed does not need to wash, except for his feet, but is completely clean. And you are clean, but not every one of you.' For he knew who was to betray him; that was why he said, 'Not all of you are clean.'

When he had washed their feet and put on his outer garments and resumed his place, he said to them, 'Do you understand what I have done to you? You call me Teacher and Lord, and you are right, for so I am. If I then, your Lord and Teacher, have washed your feet, you also ought to wash one another's feet. For I have given you an example, that you also should do just as I have done to you.'

(John 13.1–15)

We move on, now, to the next stage of our journey into the Easter mystery.

We use the word 'mystery', not because we don't have any understanding of it, as if it were a puzzle we cannot solve. No, we use the word 'mystery' in another sense: that this is the plan of God, established before all ages in God's eternal wisdom, for our salvation. Here, then, we celebrate the Mystery of Salvation, those actions of God by which we come to the fullness of life. And at the heart of this mystery is the death of Christ on the cross and his resurrection from the dead.

The Book of Exodus gives us the prefiguring of this great gift in the Passover meal of the people of Israel. The sacrifice of the lamb, by which the people are saved from death and slavery, becomes effective in their lives through sharing it as a meal, as food to be consumed.

This same pattern is made new in Christ. Now it is his blood that is poured out for us, his flesh that is eaten. He is the lamb of the new Passover, the Paschal Lamb of God.

There is in my mind a particular phrase of the New Testament. It is, I believe, a key to our celebration of this Sacred Mystery. It comes from the Book of Revelation and it is this: 'Behold, I am making all things new' (Revelation 21.5).

In the Eucharist, Jesus makes new the sacrifice of the Old Law. In the Eucharist, Jesus offers to us the gift of new life. Through our participation in the Eucharist, we are indeed made new, for, as St Paul has told us, every time we 'eat this bread and drink the cup' (1 Corinthians 11.26), we are proclaiming, here and now, the death of Christ, the death by which we are given that new life.

There is a unique and crucial character to this eating and drinking which sets it apart from all other food and drink. Normally when we eat and drink, we absorb the food we take in. It becomes part of us, part of our flesh and blood. But with the Body and Blood of Christ, it is not we who absorb the food that we receive but rather we are absorbed by it. We become part of what we receive. Through this eating and drinking we are absorbed into Christ, we become part of him, his body, the Church, his presence in the world.

> *By our sharing in the Eucharist, we become part of Christ's offering of himself to the Father*

By our sharing in the Eucharist, we become part of Christ's offering of himself to the Father. Our lives are taken up into his. We become part of his sufferings, uniting our distress and hurt with his. We become sharers in his compassion and love, able then to offer to others the compassion and love that we have ourselves received.

In all these ways he makes us new. 'Behold, I am making all things new.'

Whenever we express or find a deep sense of gratitude to God, there we see the newness of Christ. Whenever we meet suffering carried with nobility and a concern for others, there we see the newness of Christ. Whenever compassion and forgiveness flow from heart to heart across the stony landscape of life, there we know the newness of life given in Christ. This is indeed the mystery of our salvation.

The washing of the feet is the sign of the preparation we need to undergo in order to enter into this new life, this new covenant, sealed in the blood of the new Lamb. This is a washing of forgiveness, a cleansing of sin, which we all need and which is made real for us in the sacrament of Reconciliation, in Confession.

It is also a sign of the humility of the Lord who reaches out to each one of us. Let us recall the words spoken by the Lord to St Peter: 'If I do not wash you, you have no share with me.' First spoken to Peter, these words are spoken to each one of us too.

'Behold, I am making all things new.' Here, in the life, death and resurrection of Jesus Christ, is the true hope for the world, the new start for which our world is longing, the yearning of every heart, the true source of forgiveness and new life.

O Lord, by your cross and resurrection you have set us free. You are the saviour of the world. Amen.

5

This is my body

For I received from the Lord what I also delivered to you, that the Lord Jesus on the night when he was betrayed took bread, and when he had given thanks, he broke it, and said, 'This is my body which is for you. Do this in remembrance of me.' In the same way also he took the cup, after supper, saying, 'This cup is the new covenant in my blood. Do this, as often as you drink it, in remembrance of me.' For as often as you eat this bread and drink the cup, you proclaim the Lord's death until he comes.

(1 Corinthians 11.23–26)

At every stage of our journey through Holy Week, this is the single reality we celebrate: the gift of the total love of Jesus for us, a love flowing from the deepest reality, from the very being of God, which Jesus, the Son of God, makes visible in our midst.

We have witnessed the manifestation of his love in his washing of the disciples' feet. We witness it again now in his handing over to them his Precious Body and Blood in the supper they share in anticipation of his sacrifice on the cross.

Both these actions of Jesus are immersed in the things of the body. In the first, he washes the feet, the flesh and blood, of his disciples. In the second, he gives himself entirely. He gives his flesh and blood, his bodily reality, in death on the cross, in the sacrament of the altar. In this way, Jesus transforms our way of understanding our bodily reality.

Jesus transforms our way of understanding our bodily reality

Our bodies are precious; they are the work of God's hands; they are the temples of the Holy Spirit. Yet we often experience our bodies as a source of trouble, of temptation, of pain and of suffering. We have been tempted to distrust and even hate our bodily reality. We hear reports of young people becoming increasingly dismayed and preoccupied by the shape of their bodies, struggling to accept themselves under the pressure of social conformity.

Such thoughts and feelings can easily become lodged in our hearts and flow from there into our attitudes and actions. But to follow this pathway, to harbour such feelings in our hearts, is to fail to see the work of God and the gifts Christ brings.

We saw earlier how the wonderful work of our redemption, accomplished by Christ in his passion, can be understood through the image of Moses bringing forth living water from the rock in the desert. We can see in that rock the hardness and waywardness of our hearts, which in turn make our bodies to be like stone. Instead of being central to loving God and one another, our bodies become barriers. Only when Christ strikes our hearts with the staff of his grace does that hardness break open and do our bodies become what God created them to be: channels of life-giving compassion and love.

What is that hardness of our hearts?

Think of the store of past offences that we often harbour within our hearts. This is our hardness of heart. How often we return to that store to refresh within us a sense of resentment and bitterness.

Think of the energy we can put into pondering our desire for revenge against those we believe have belittled us. We want to even up the score, and that desire coarsens and hardens our hearts.

Think of our habit of turning away from those in need, of averting our eyes lest their need touch our hearts and we have to respond.

Think of the weariness of heart that we so often feel, saying to ourselves that we have done enough already and there is no point in doing more.

Think, again, of the ways in which, from time to time, we view ourselves with disgust and lose heart about our own worthiness.

Think of all the other ways, which each of us knows well, in which our hearts have become hard – as hard as rock – and from which we are not really ready to turn away.

But if we cry out in repentance and faith to the Lord, we know he will take away the heart of stone from within our bodies and give us a heart of flesh instead. When he strikes the rock of our heart with the staff of his love, living water flows within us and we may truly be his disciples.

This he can do, both today and every day, through the power of his sacrifice. This sacrifice of Christ, the offering of his Body and Blood, never ceases. It is always available to us. Every time we find within our-selves a hardness of heart, we can return to him, open our hearts to him and allow him to restore in us the great gift of love.

O Lord, may we draw from this mystery the fullness of love and know the lightness of a loving heart, finding fulfilment in the generous service of all around us. Amen.

6

Love one another

When he had gone out, Jesus said, 'Now is the Son
of Man glorified, and God is glorified in him. If God
is glorified in him, God will also glorify him in himself, and glorify him at once. Little children, yet a
little while I am with you. You will seek me, and just
as I said to the Jews, so now I also say to you, "Where
I am going you cannot come." A new commandment
I give to you, that you love one another: just as I have
loved you, you also are to love one another. By this
all people will know that you are my disciples, if you
have love for one another.'

(John 13.31–35)

We are now entering the time of the Passion. In a
short time, this band of disciples, gathered round their
Master, will be engulfed by darkness and terror. In
the darkness, a traitor from their midst will betray
the Lord with a clamour of soldiers and swords. Jesus
will be snatched away. Their world will fall apart.

How will they survive without him?

There is a one-word answer that occurs in the title of this day: Maundy Thursday. These days, 'Maundy' is often associated with the gift given by the monarch: the Maundy money. But the origin of the word is older. 'Maundy' comes from the Latin word *mandatum*, meaning 'command'.

Jesus leaves with his disciples a double command: two interconnected actions, which we also are called to obey.

The first command comes from the record of the Last Supper that we thought about earlier: 'Do this in remembrance of me.'

I wonder if, in the entire history of humanity, any command has ever been so widely or consistently obeyed: in cathedrals and great churches, in prison cells, out in fields, on mountain tops and before crowds of millions. In most countries on earth, this command has been obeyed. And Jesus, he who was snatched away from us, is with us.

The second command, or *mandatum*, is inseparable from the first. It is the command to love and serve one another, as symbolized in the washing of feet: 'If I then, your Lord and Teacher, have washed your feet, you also ought to wash one another's feet' (John 13.14).

In this Gospel passage, St John leaves us in no doubt: Jesus knew what he was about. We know this from phrases such as, 'Jesus knew that his hour had come', 'Jesus, knowing that the Father had given all things into his hands', 'he knew who was to betray him' and 'he said to them, "Do you understand . . . ?"' (John 13.1, 3, 11, 12).

Washing feet was the duty of a slave. Here it is an offering of love. While the world is full of people standing on their own dignity, in Jesus we see the only lasting greatness: the greatness of love, humility and service.

This, then, is what Jesus commands: 'Do this in remembrance of me', and 'Just as I have loved you, you also are to love one another.'

In Jesus we see the only lasting greatness: the greatness of love, humility and service

These two commands are inseparable. Service flows from true participation in the Eucharist. Service is the gateway through which we must pass in order to be truly part of this eucharistic celebration.

33

Yet so often they are pulled apart. Service without any reference to the source of that loving service, God himself, is service that may indeed be nobly generous yet it will not reveal, or witness to, whence it ultimately flows. Celebrating the Eucharist without attending to the love and service that should flow from it is a hollow and shallow form of celebration.

In the light of faith, we see that these two commands of Jesus should always go hand in hand. Jesus, the Eternal Word in our flesh, shows us the wholeness of human life, a service that springs from the wonder and praise of God, and a Eucharist validated and made vibrant by selfless service to those most in need.

O God who has called us to participate in this most sacred Supper, grant, we pray, that we may draw from so great a mystery the fullness of charity and of life. Amen.

Part 3

VICTORY FROM REJECTION
(GOOD FRIDAY)

7

Jesus gives his life

Jesus . . . went out with his disciples across the Kidron Valley, where there was a garden, which he and his disciples entered. Now Judas, who betrayed him, also knew the place, for Jesus often met there with his disciples. So Judas, having procured a band of soldiers and some officers from the chief priests and the Pharisees, went there with lanterns and torches and weapons. Then Jesus, knowing all that would happen to him, came forward and said to them, 'Whom do you seek?' They answered him, 'Jesus of Nazareth.' Jesus said to them, 'I am he.' Judas, who betrayed him, was standing with them. When Jesus said to them, 'I am he', they drew back and fell to the ground . . .

Then they led Jesus from the house of Caiaphas to the governor's headquarters. It was early morning. They themselves did not enter the governor's head-quarters, so that they would not be defiled, but could eat the Passover. So Pilate went outside to them and said, 'What accusation do you bring against this man?'

They answered him, 'If this man were not doing evil, we would not have delivered him over to you.' Pilate said to them, 'Take him yourselves and judge him by your own law.' The Jews said to him, 'It is not lawful for us to put anyone to death.' This was to fulfil the word that Jesus had spoken to show by what kind of death he was going to die.

So Pilate entered his headquarters again and called Jesus and said to him, 'Are you the King of the Jews?' Jesus answered, 'Do you say this of your own accord, or did others say it to you about me?' Pilate answered, 'Am I a Jew? Your own nation and the chief priests have delivered you over to me. What have you done?' Jesus answered, 'My kingdom is not of this world. If my kingdom were of this world, my servants would have been fighting, that I might not be delivered over to the Jews. But my kingdom is not from the world.' Then Pilate said to him, 'So you are a king?' Jesus answered, 'You say that I am a king. For this purpose I was born and for this purpose I have come into the world – to bear witness to the truth. Everyone who is of the truth listens to my voice.' Pilate said to him, 'What is truth?' . . .

Then Pilate took Jesus and flogged him. And the soldiers twisted together a crown of thorns and put it on his head and arrayed him in a purple robe. They came up to him, saying, 'Hail, King of the Jews!' and struck him with their hands. Pilate went out again and said to them, 'See, I am bringing him out to you that you may know that I find no guilt in him.' So Jesus came out, wearing the crown of thorns and the purple robe. Pilate said to them, 'Behold the man!'

(John 18.1–6, 28–38; 19.1–5)

On Good Friday we stand before our crucified Lord, contemplating his death on the cross for each one of us, for us all.

His death is a fact of history. The Gospel gives a clear account of what actually happened. It is not a story told for our encouragement. Yet this single event is of huge, unique significance. It opens for us a horizon on to eternity. It transforms our entire understanding of ourselves and of our destiny.

Pope Francis has encouraged us to be a people who want always to point to a horizon of beauty. He wants us to invite others to gaze on this same beauty. He wants us to invite them to our special beauty spot. It is here, at the foot of the cross. Yet to understand the beauty of this place, to see beyond its horrendous cruelty, we must look closely, with a rare openness of heart.

In St John's account of the passion, we are told four times of events that took place to fulfil the Scriptures (John 17.12; 19.24, 28, 36). Clearly, here a greater purpose than the death of one man is being worked out. That man, Jesus, himself said, 'For this purpose I was born and for this purpose I have come into the world – to bear witness to the truth' (John 18.37). So here, in this event, a great truth is being told. And we search for the lasting beauty of that truth.

Pilate said to the people, 'Behold the man!' The same is said to us today: 'Behold the man!' But, we ask, who exactly is this man?

Jesus tells us. He says, 'I am he.' And, at these words, the people 'drew back and fell to the ground'. Why? Because the words Jesus has used are the very words used by God himself, to identify himself to Moses: literally 'I AM WHO I AM' (Exodus 3.14).

And so we see that the Eternal Word of God, in our flesh, came to be hanging on the cross. From the very beginning of the Gospel, John has made that clear: 'And the Word became flesh and dwelt among us, and we have seen his glory, glory as of the only Son from the

Father, full of grace and truth' (John 1.14). It is this Word who hangs in bodily death before us. It is his glory and his truth within the reality of death that we can now begin to see!

How do we see here this glory, grace and truth? Where is the beauty in this crucifixion?

Good Friday exemplifies the history of our humanity in all its horror and destructiveness. The One on the cross, the Eternal Word through whom all things were made, takes to himself, as only he could do, the sufferings of every person, from the first Adam to this very day. He soaks into himself all the anger and sin of our humanity. And it renders him disfigured: 'his appearance was so marred, beyond human semblance', as the Prophet Isaiah said (52.14). In him we see the terrible truth of our human condition, all our awful history of damage and destruction of each other, of the ways we disfigure and deface all that is good and beautiful.

Yet already a new horizon is dawning, because we know that in the person of Jesus we do not see a helpless victim, but rather one who willingly gives his life, accepting the cross and embracing all its horror. In him we see love expressing itself unto the very end, faithful, paying the ultimate price, never wavering from love's embrace, never saying, 'That's enough, I will take no more!' In Jesus, we see the beauty of limitless love.

In Jesus, we see the beauty of limitless love

In him we sense, even now, the love of the Father and the Holy Spirit embracing this broken form, our broken history, and drawing it into its new future, its true form, its fulfilment. The crucified Jesus, then, is a statement of the truth of our terrible reality bathed in a redeeming light. This is the beauty of love's final depth.

The cross is a horizon of beauty, an opening to the pure light of God. This is its hidden truth, because here we see love in its moment of true victory over its two enemies: betrayal and death. Neither can belittle or destroy this love. It withstands the ultimate test. This love does not end and so its beauty shines forth. This is love, and life, which even in its final emptiness conquers death itself.

All beauty, if it is not to be superficial or fleeting, must overcome all that opposes it. True beauty endures. It is always more than skin deep. Here, in Jesus, in this one man, is the whole of God's eternal and created beauty: the beauty of love overcoming all limitations. Here, in Jesus, we see the eternal plan of God for all his creation. It is stunning and absolutely compelling.

At the end of Good Friday lies the glory and victory of beauty itself, the beauty of God which we are all called to share as our eternal destiny. That is our joy, our victory, our redemption!

Our pathway through life is a journey to the fullness of beauty. So our moral guide is that of rejecting all that can again damage or deform the beauty within us.

On this day of our salvation, let us praise God in the beauty of holiness, now and for ever. Amen.

8

The loving sacrifice

From then on Pilate sought to release him, but the Jews cried out, 'If you release this man, you are not Caesar's friend. Everyone who makes himself a king opposes Caesar.' So when Pilate heard these words, he brought Jesus out and sat down on the judgement seat at a place called The Stone Pavement, and in Aramaic Gabbatha. Now it was the day of Preparation of the Passover. It was about the sixth hour. He said to the Jews, 'Behold your King!' They cried out, 'Away with him, away with him, crucify him!' Pilate said to them, 'Shall I crucify your King?' The chief priests answered, 'We have no king but Caesar.' So he delivered him over to them to be crucified.

So they took Jesus, and he went out, bearing his own cross, to the place called The Place of a Skull, which in Aramaic is called Golgotha. There they crucified him, and with him two others, one on either side, and Jesus between them . . .

When the soldiers had crucified Jesus, they took his garments and divided them into four parts, one part for each soldier; also his tunic. But the tunic was seamless, woven in one piece from top to bottom, so they said to one another, 'Let us not tear it, but cast lots for it to see whose it shall be.' This was to fulfil the Scripture which says,

'They divided my garments among them,
  and for my clothing they cast lots.'

So the soldiers did these things, but standing by the cross of Jesus were his mother and his mother's sister, Mary the wife of Clopas, and Mary Magdalene. When Jesus saw his mother and the disciple whom he loved standing nearby, he said to his mother, 'Woman, behold, your son!' Then he said to the disciple, 'Behold, your mother!' And from that hour the disciple took her to his own home.

After this, Jesus, knowing that all was now finished, said (to fulfil the Scripture), 'I thirst.' A jar full of sour wine stood there, so they put a sponge full of the sour wine on a hyssop branch and held it to his mouth. When Jesus had received the sour wine, he said, 'It is finished', and he bowed his head and gave up his spirit.

(John 19.12–18, 23–30)

As we gaze on Jesus hanging on the cross, we acknow-
ledge him to be our high priest, the one who presents
himself, in his emptiness, to his loving Father on our
behalf. In this moment, as in every moment of prayer,
we unite ourselves to Christ, that we may become part
of his offering, his prayer to God, who is the same
God and Father of us all.

The Letter to the Hebrews is so encouraging. 'Since
then we have a great high priest who has passed
through the heavens, Jesus, the Son of God, let us
hold fast our confession' (Hebrews 4.14). Let us allow
those words to strengthen our faith, and particularly
our faith in Jesus, the Lord, who is now eternally in
the presence of his Father interceding for us in his
everlasting priesthood.

There are so many things on which we could ponder. But here are two, briefly put, that can direct and
guide us in our own prayer as a priestly people.

On the cross, Jesus cries out, 'I thirst', and he is
given vinegar, sour wine, to drink. Here are strong
echoes of the Old Testament, and of the Psalms in
particular. In Psalm 69 the just man, in his suffering,
laments that 'for my thirst they gave me sour wine to
drink' (verse 21). Jesus is that just man. He is every

just person exposed to suffering and distress. Here we are also reminded of the image of the vineyard. God plants a vineyard on a fertile hillside, but all it yields are wild grapes. As Pope Benedict says, 'The vineyard of Israel fails to yield for God the noble fruit of justice, which is grounded in love. It yields the sour grapes of man who is concerned only for himself.'[1]

Let us not yield only sour grapes. Let us rather present the Lord with the gift of forgiveness of those who have wronged us and compassion to those who are burdened. Let us thirst for the beauty of God's truth just as Jesus thirsts for us to come to him. In this way we play our part in consecrating our world to God today.

In his last moments Jesus also cries out, 'It is finished.' It is accomplished. His great task is complete. All that remains is for the Father to complete his task: that of raising Jesus to new life.

What exactly is the task of Jesus? It is that of bringing the whole world, summed up in his body, to the Father. He does this completely, for he is truly both God and man, the Word through whom all things are

---

1 Joseph Ratzinger, Pope Benedict XVI, *Jesus of Nazareth: Holy Week* (San Francisco: Ignatius Press, 2011), p. 218.

made. In this way, Jesus consecrates our world. As priest he hands it over to God, right unto the end, until all is accomplished. And the sign of it being accomplished is the piercing of his side so that the last drops of blood and water are shed.

This happens at the very hour when the lambs of the Jewish liturgy are being slaughtered in the temple. In Jesus, that form of worship comes to an end, for he is now the Lamb of God who takes away from the world the ultimate effects of our sin. In this way, too, he is our high priest, and in him all our prayers for forgiveness and mercy find their answer. This is now the new, true worship, for now his body is the new temple, and, most remarkably, we are now that body.

My brothers and sisters, here is the greatness of our calling: to be the body of Christ in our world; to be the focus of true prayer, the point at which all the world's troubles are raised up before God in union with Jesus. This is the great dignity of being a priestly people called to consecrate the world to God through lives of holiness and faith.

So whenever we approach the cross to venerate the Lord, let us keep in mind the words from the Letter to the Hebrews: 'Let us then with confidence draw near to the throne of grace, that we may receive mercy and find grace to help in time of need' (Hebrews 4.16).

This is our true place: at the foot of the cross, ready to venerate our Lord, to receive him with love and to be those who will continue in our lives his work of bringing all things to God for healing and redemption.

The death of Christ restores in us the gift of divine love. Through the death of Christ, love is infused into our souls by the Holy Spirit, the love that is of God, the love by which we love God, above all things, and our neighbours too, as ourselves. The cross, then, in its power of restoring love, is the wellspring of our life in Christ.

> *Through the death of Christ, love is infused into our souls*

Loving God, may we all embrace the cross of Christ in love and true devotion. Amen.

9

The glorious victory

Who has believed what he has heard from us?
And to whom has the arm of the LORD been revealed?
For he grew up before him like a young plant,
and like a root out of dry ground;
he had no form or majesty that we should look at him,
and no beauty that we should desire him.
He was despised and rejected by men;
a man of sorrows, and acquainted with grief;
and as one from whom men hide their faces
he was despised, and we esteemed him not.
Surely he has borne our griefs
and carried our sorrows;
yet we esteemed him stricken,
smitten by God, and afflicted.
But he was wounded for our transgressions;
he was crushed for our iniquities;
upon him was the chastisement that brought us peace,
and with his stripes we are healed.
All we like sheep have gone astray;

we have turned – every one – to his own way;
and the LORD has laid on him
the iniquity of us all.
He was oppressed, and he was afflicted,
yet he opened not his mouth;
like a lamb that is led to the slaughter,
and like a sheep that before its shearers is silent,
so he opened not his mouth.
By oppression and judgement he was taken away;
and as for his generation, who considered
that he was cut off out of the land of the living,
stricken for the transgression of my people?
And they made his grave with the wicked
and with a rich man in his death,
although he had done no violence,
and there was no deceit in his mouth.
Yet it was the will of the LORD to crush him;
he has put him to grief;
when his soul makes an offering for guilt,
he shall see his offspring; he shall prolong his days;
the will of the LORD shall prosper in his hand.
Out of the anguish of his soul he shall see and be
satisfied;
by his knowledge shall the righteous one, my servant,
make many to be accounted righteous,

and he shall bear their iniquities.
Therefore I will divide him a portion with the many,
and he shall divide the spoil with the strong,
because he poured out his soul to death
and was numbered with the transgressors;
yet he bore the sin of many,
and makes intercession for the transgressors.

(Isaiah 53)

This is the reality of Good Friday, the day on which we come face to face with suffering and with death. It is, of course, the suffering and death of Jesus that we contemplate. But we do well to have in mind our own too: the suffering that marks our own lives and the death that we shall certainly experience.

The Prophet Isaiah explores the destructiveness of suffering. 'He had no form or majesty', 'no beauty that we should desire him', 'a man of sorrows, and acquainted with grief'. These phrases resonate with our experience of those we know who have been struck with great suffering either in years of strength or in the time of old age. The inner paradoxes of our fallen human nature, the juxtaposition of our nobility with the great suffering that can strike us, are vividly portrayed in this reading.

On Good Friday these words are applied to Jesus who, although the eternal Son of God, embraces human suffering and makes it his own. But we also learn that he does so in a particular way: exactly because he is true God and true man. He who is totally innocent bears this suffering on our behalf.

And as we stand at the foot of the cross, we see him not only accepting this suffering but also being overwhelmed by it, crushed and falling, like every human being, into the pit of death.

Suffering and death in our lives are like the rock in the desert which confronted the people of God on their journey to the promised land at a time when they were parched with thirst and rebellious in heart. Suffering is like a rock that slowly crushes the life out of us. Death is seen as the ultimate, impenetrable rock, beyond which nothing can be glimpsed.

Yet the promise of God, enacted in that desert, is that he will strike this rock and, from its barrenness, bring forth a stream of living water.

As we stand at the foot of the cross, we know, in faith, that this is so. Out of the suffering and death of Jesus a glorious victory is being born. Out of this rock, life-giving water will indeed pour forth. For

Jesus, in the power of the Holy
Spirit, will strike the rock of suffering and death with the staff of his
cross. Then, we know, this death is
split open, destroyed, giving way to
new, everlasting life.

*Out of the
suffering and
death of Jesus
a glorious victory
is being born*

This is the greatness of Good Friday. We know the
corrosive power of suffering. We may witness it within
our own family or circle of friends: prolonged suffering
and increasing incapacity can sap our energy and our
belief. We know, too, how totally death can destroy
human hope. Everything we have achieved, the success
of work, the bonds of love and friendship, appear to
be pointless in the face of death, for death delivers only
oblivion. In human terms, everything is lost.

Yet here, in the shadow of the cross, a new light is
cast. If Jesus suffers in this way out of love, in innocence,
then there is some new purpose to be found. His suffering is a gift that is acceptable to his loving Father, a
gift of love that unlocks for all the freely flowing tenderness, mercy and compassion of the heart of God.
I can join my suffering to his. Then my suffering, too,
enriches the flow of mercy for all. In this way, in Christ,
the rock face of suffering is broken open. Suffering

faithfully borne in union with Christ becomes part of the mysterious movement of love across the face of the earth, touching the hearts of so many.

Here, in the shadow of the cross, a new light is also cast on the reality of death. No longer does it bring final oblivion, but rather it is the final door through which we must pass. In uttering the words, 'It is finished', Jesus heralds in a new era. In his dying he casts death aside. In his rising from the dead he breaks open the rock of death until it becomes a triumphal arch through which all can pass who cling to him. This is our faith. This is our sure hope. This is the goodness of Good Friday.

Let us, then, hold steady before the cross of Christ. Here we can look death in the eye and embrace our dying Saviour, who alone delivers us from its cold embrace.

O Christ, we thank you for the victory you accomplished for us through your life-giving death on the cross. Amen.

Part 4

LIFE FROM THE TOMB
(EASTER SUNDAY)

10

Jesus is risen!

Now on the first day of the week Mary Magdalene came to the tomb early, while it was still dark, and saw that the stone had been taken away from the tomb. So she ran and went to Simon Peter and the other disciple, the one whom Jesus loved, and said to them, 'They have taken the Lord out of the tomb, and we do not know where they have laid him.' So Peter went out with the other disciple, and they were going towards the tomb. Both of them were running together, but the other disciple outran Peter and reached the tomb first. And stooping to look in, he saw the linen cloths lying there, but he did not go in. Then Simon Peter came, following him, and went into the tomb. He saw the linen cloths lying there, and the face cloth, which had been on Jesus' head, not lying with the linen cloths but folded up in a place by itself. Then the other disciple, who had reached the tomb first, also went in, and he saw and believed; for as yet they did not understand the

Scripture, that he must rise from the dead. Then the disciples went back to their homes.

(John 20.1–10)

Mary Magdalene is running to Simon Peter with astonishing news; Peter and John dash back to the tomb to see for themselves, the young John outstripping the older man. Peter is quick to become a witness to these events: to the preaching and miracles of Jesus, to his death by 'hanging on a tree' and to his being raised to life. God, he says, 'commanded us to preach to the people . . . that everyone who believes in him receives forgiveness of sins through his name' (Acts 10.39, 42–43).

Talk of sin is not always popular – unless we are talking about other people's sins. Then we can't get enough of it. That's what really sells newspapers! But to appreciate the message of this great Christian feast we have to begin with our own sense of need.

A self-sufficient soul has no sense of Easter.

Mary Magdalene, Peter, John and the others knew better. They knew that in Jesus they had met someone who opened up a way of life beyond the pettiness, jealousies and violence that mark and mar our human nature. Then he was executed, and the dream vanished like mist. But with his resurrection from the dead, all is alive again – literally alive in a new and revolutionary way.

To appreciate the message of this great Christian feast we have to begin with our own sense of need

Jesus goes beyond everything we know for ourselves. Most importantly, he goes beyond our sense of justice. We know all about 'an eye for an eye'. We know all about 'making them pay'. But here an innocent person pays an exorbitant price so that we who are guilty may receive a priceless blessing. Far from exacting human justice, this judge steps in to take the punishment himself so that we may walk free and forgiven. And to demonstrate its truth, he bursts out of the tomb of death.

What does all this mean? St Paul tells us plainly. Here, he says, is a glimpse of the glory that belongs to all of us. 'When Christ who is your life appears, then you also will appear with him in glory' (Colossians 3.4). We go from forgiveness to fulfilment, from the status of a sinner to one of sharing in the glory of Christ. This comes to us only slowly. Only by being close to Christ; by learning his Way; by conforming our thinking, our speaking and our acting to his, can the change begin to come about. It is the work of the Holy Spirit, the breath of the Spirit within us – inspiration!

This is the message that inspires our finest efforts. This is the message that brings us hope: hope that the vision of life embodied in the risen Christ can find its place in ours, despite all the sin and failure that we know so well; hope that with all the inspiration we can receive we can fashion a society in which graciousness is visible and forgiveness forthcoming; hope that in our homes today we will radiate the joy of the risen Christ.

Alleluia is our song. Christ is truly risen from the dead, we know; Victorious king, thy mercy show! Amen.

11

The one who goes before

For we know that if the tent that is our earthly home
is destroyed, we have a building from God, a house
not made with hands, eternal in the heavens. For in
this tent we groan, longing to put on our heavenly
dwelling, if indeed by putting it on we may not be
found naked. For while we are still in this tent, we
groan, being burdened – not that we would be
unclothed, but that we would be further clothed, so
that what is mortal may be swallowed up by life. He
who has prepared us for this very thing is God, who
has given us the Spirit as a guarantee . . .

For the love of Christ controls us, because we
have concluded this: that one has died for all, therefore all have died; and he died for all, that those who
live might no longer live for themselves but for him
who for their sake died and was raised.

(2 Corinthians 5.1–5, 14–15)

Easter is full of promise because the one who embodied our death, who took on the burden of our sins, has been raised from the dead by the power of the Holy Spirit. We proclaim: Alleluia, He is Risen!

With his rising from the dead, we are given the chance to rise from our sins. In his rising from the dead, we see beyond the shroud of death.

We know the darkness of death. We watch the work of death every day in the ceaseless work of war in zones of conflict around the world. We watch the work of death in the disintegration of bodies and minds through the sicknesses that rob us of our loved ones and carry us to our end. In Jesus, the ultimate effects of these are overcome, for in him God fulfils his promise to bring all creation to a new fulfilment, a new and glorious life.

But death casts a long shadow. So many good things of this life escape us sooner or later, coming to an untimely end. We know what gives us joy and satisfaction. But they do not last. Friendships die and may even turn bitter; holidays come to an end and routine returns. Even the best of parties finishes, and sometimes all that is left is the hangover! So where does lasting joy abide? What is it that makes life truly worthwhile?

Into this scene comes this new and startling light. It is like a new cosmic blaze, a new dawn, shedding a powerful and warming light which we can describe only in terms of absolute love. Yes, it is the light of love that radiates from this tomb. It is the light of unquenchable love, an unfailing love which gradually overcomes the separations, the disintegrations and the little deaths with which we live, day by day.

Often the coming of Jesus into this world is spoken of as his leaving his Godhead to enter into our mortal world. His rising from the dead is seen as his return to the glory of God. And that is true. But, sometimes, hidden in this thought is the idea that Jesus took on our messy humanity as an unfortunate condition of his mission in our world, and on his return he leaves all its messiness behind. But this is not so. Jesus comes to our world as the act of God's love. He enters our flesh not as a burden to his Godhead but as an expression of the deepest nature of all that God has made, for God saw it and it was very good (Genesis 1.31). And in returning to his Father, Jesus does not strip away his humanity as if it were a source of impurity. No, he rises in and with his body. He carries it home. And with his risen body he goes before us, carrying home all of the created order, which has its being through him, the Eternal Word.

> *With his risen body he goes before us, carrying home all of the created order*

Jesus, we are told, loves 'his own' even to the end (John 13.1), even though 'his own' would not accept him (John 1.11). But in his rising from the dead, in his own home-coming, each one of us also finds our way home opened and clearly marked out. We may often be tempted to think of our flesh, our humanity, as the part of us that we must go beyond and which we must somehow reject. But Jesus does not do that. Rather, he raises it up to new life.

Only in this light do we see our physical world correctly. Only in this light, the light of our eternal destiny, do we see our true glory, and the glory of our bodily selves. In God's eyes we never lose our dignity, not even when the human body is stripped and debased, as it is so often for reasons of violence and exploitation. Here is a human body raised from the dead, raised from a broken and deformed state and entered into its true and eternal glory. And in that body we all share. For this is the body of our Lord, shared with us in every Eucharist, when he takes us into himself that he may, in due time, take us to our heavenly home.

So this Easter, let us be restored in our Christian confidence. Those who belittle faith and ridicule the things we cherish do so from a distance, with little understanding of the true reality of a relationship with the Lord. We know better because we live these truths of faith; we know and love our Lord and rejoice that he has gone before us, victorious in his resurrection and new life.

May our hearts be full of joy as we greet our risen Lord and accept again his gracious invitation to live in him, to pray in him, to rise again in him, in God's good time. Amen.

12

The new creation

From now on, therefore, we regard no one according to the flesh. Even though we once regarded Christ according to the flesh, we regard him thus no longer. Therefore, if anyone is in Christ, he is a new creation. The old has passed away; behold, the new has come. All this is from God, who through Christ reconciled us to himself and gave us the ministry of reconciliation; that is, in Christ God was reconciling the world to himself, not counting their trespasses against them, and entrusting to us the message of reconciliation.

(2 Corinthians 5.16–19)

We read earlier from St John's account of how, after finding the tomb of Jesus to be empty, Mary Magdalene runs to her friends, the disciples, and how Peter and John set off running to the tomb in response. Peter, puffing and out of breath, is easily overtaken by the young John. John arrives first, but he stands back to allow Peter to be the first to enter. For Peter is to be the prime witness, the first to speak formally of the resurrection of Jesus, as we see in the Acts of the Apostles (2.32).

Yet it is John who first recognizes the truth of what they have both seen. Here we see again that love recognizes things the mind is slow to grasp. For this is not just about an empty tomb; not just about a missing body. This is the place of the greatest story ever told. Jesus is risen! A man has come to new life after the totality of death.

But that is not all. This man is the Son of God, God from God, Light from Light, the Eternal Word. What has been done by God – for only God can do this – has been done in our flesh so that we may share its fruit, its victory. In a phrase: life now rules where death once reigned.

Our task is to apply this to our own lives and to live by that new life. So where, in our lives, does death reign?

There is often a darkness in our hearts, whenever we harbour destructiveness and bitterness, a lack of forgiveness or a desire to have our revenge. There is a harshness in our world, marked at times by cynicism, by corrosive mistrust, by a lack of forgiveness. There is the power of suffering that touches so many of us. There is the presence of sin, which pulls towards repeating behaviours that harm and hurt others and ourselves at the same time. Then there is the darkness of death itself which offers us, so it seems, nothing but oblivion.

Christ's victory is over each one of these.

Our hearts can share in the love that flows from him, from the source of the very life of God. He entered our world, our city, and carried into every corner his grace and his love, even to the ultimate measure of the cross. He carried our suffering so that when we are suffering we may be united to him. His victory over death opens for us the escape from death's cold embrace through the unbreakable promise of life after death, for all eternity.

Our faith in Christ and his victory over death give us the true meaning of our lives today. This faith is prompted in our hearts not so much by a fear of death as by a quest for life. Without this faith, so

> *His victory over death opens for us the escape from death's cold embrace*

much is missing from life. For me, all that gives me lasting joy, all that really moves my soul and inspires hope and confidence within me, all that is marked by true beauty, is rooted in the mystery of God, and in the mystery of God made visible in Christ.

Without that faith, life would be shaped only by the meaning I can give it. Without such faith we can become afraid of living. Indeed, in pain and loneliness, or in even the prospect of pain and loneliness, life, for some, loses its purpose.

But life, in itself, is a gift, not a possession: a gift of God, not a self-made acquisition. In Christ's resurrection we glimpse the full splendour of that gift – body and spirit – in its true meaning for today and its true destiny for tomorrow.

In the wonderful words of St Paul:

Therefore, if anyone is in Christ, he is a new creation. The old has passed away; behold, the new has come.

(2 Corinthians 5.17)

Easter is a great festival of human life, in which we celebrate the gift of Christ conquering corruption and death. This Easter gift is no fleeting moment, but a radically new creation: a new horizon by which to set our course; a new way of life for us to pursue; a new grace and power by which we can live.

I urge you to return often to its source, to Christ, to the Church and her sacraments.

May this Easter be a fresh start for us all, as we go forward in the love of Christ and in the grace and power of his Spirit. Amen.